Pandemic Haiku

Also by Robert Epstein:

A Congregation of Cows: Moo Haiku

A Walk around Spring Lake: Haiku

(Editor) All the Way Home: Aging in Haiku

(Editor) *Beyond the Grave: Contemporary Afterlife Haiku*

Checkout Time is Noon: Death Awareness Haiku

Checkout Time is Soon: More Death Awareness Haiku

(Editor) *Dreams Wander On: Contemporary Poems of Death Awareness*

(Co-Editor with Miriam Wald) *Every Chicken, Cow, Fish and Frog: Animal Rights Haiku*

Free to Dance Forever: Mourning Haiku for My Mother

Haiku Days of Remembrance: In Honor of My Father

Haiku Edge: New and Selected Poems

Haiku Forest Afterlife

Healing into Haiku: On Illness and Pain

(Second author with Stacy Taylor) *Living Well with a Hidden Disability*

Nothing is Empty: A Whole Haiku World

(Editor) *Now This: Contemporary Poems of Beginnings, Renewals, and Firsts*

Poor Robert's Almanac: Little Observations on Life

(With Stacy Taylor) *Suffering Buddha: The Zen Way Beyond Health and Illness*

(Editor) *The Breath of Surrender: A Collection of Recovery-Oriented Haiku*

(Compiler with Sherry Phillips) *The Natural Man: A Thoreau Anthology*

Reckoning with Winter: A Haiku Hailstorm

(Editor) The Helping Hand Haiku Anthology (Including Senryu, Tanka and Haiga)

(Editor) *The Sacred in Contemporary Haiku*

(Editor) The Signature Haiku Anthology (Including Senryu & Tanka)

(Editor) *The Temple Bell Stops: Contemporary Poems of Grief, Loss and Change*

(Editor) *They Gave Us Life: Celebrating Mothers, Fathers, & Others in Haiku*

Turkey Heaven: Animal Rights Haiku

Turning the Page to Old: Haiku & Senryu

Pandemic Haiku:
Living through COVID-19

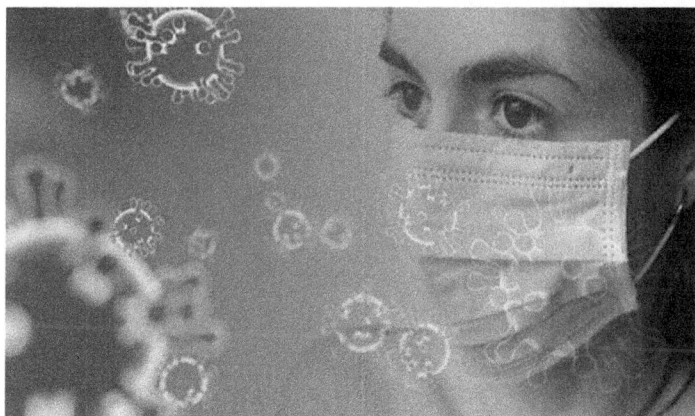

Robert Epstein

Middle Island Press
2020

To

Everyone

Table of Contents

Acknowledgments

I am always happy to express appreciation for family and friends: Louise and Mel Adler, Janet Amptman, Kathy DiNapoli, Kim Durham, Durham, David J. and Nancy Eagle, Debbie Edwards, Martin Epstein, Clara Knopfler, Joy McCall, Alyson and Anthony Nicolosi, Sherry Phillips, Judy Rader, Katherine Raine, Rocco Randazzo David H. Rosen, Wendy Etsuko Siu, Lillian Schwartz, CarrieAnn Thunell, Joan Vander Ryk, and Erika Zarco. Jay Schlesinger, Sophie Soltani, Stacy Taylor and Miriam Wald ––in whom I have confided for so many years ––deserve my deepest gratitude.

One of the poems originally appeared in the online journal, *Halku Page*; I wish to thank the editor of that publication. With much gratitude, I want to acknowledge Christina Taylor of Middle Island Press for all her help in bringing this poetry collection to print.

Preface

> Overcoming ignorance is the
> road to recovery from pandemics.

~ Anonymous

I am not an infectious disease specialist nor a politician who makes policy. Rather, I am a haiku poet who records my lived experience through the medium of poetry. Haiku (as well as senryu) is a primary means for *bearing the unbearable* and the novel coronavirus pandemic falls squarely into this category.

In the face of a crisis, it is virtually impossible to see beyond the flames, the flooding or, in this case, the staggering number of confirmed cases as well as the casualties. There is no point in trying to pretend I am sitting with equanimity on a meditation cushion, chanting OM twelve hours a day. No, I am translating my fear, sadness, relief, worry, love, loneliness, helplessness and a host of other emotional reactions into poetry that others might be able to relate to. Invariably, one will encounter redundancy since sheltering-in-place and listening to daily news briefings have a repetitiveness to them. Too, I must invariably repeat myself in the process of brailling my way through the dark caves that is the coronavirus pandemic in search of light, freedom and fresh air. For this, I hope the reader will forgive me; perchance I am mirroring his or her own experience.

There is so much uncertainty woven into life. Most of the time we cope with this uncertainty through the pursuit of pleasure and distraction. But, the pandemic has thrown a gigantic monkey wrench into the works. All of us have been thrust into an urgent need to protect ourselves from a virulent virus that could force the most vulnerable onto ventilators while the rest of us worry about our livelihoods and futures. Only those most in denial can continue on nonchalantly or in defiance.

In short, this pandemic has cut through the *consensus trance* that enables most people to lumber through their daily lives without a thought about death and dying. The coronavirus has shattered the bubble we live in: the daily death toll has made sure of this.

The US economy has been decimated by the pandemic, which has resulted in massive job losses. The ramifications of this are real, extensive and heartbreaking. They should not be minimized. That said, as terrible and far-reaching as the financial hardships are, the economy can be revived following a recession. A dead person cannot be brought back to life. Others may disagree——especially in cases where those in despair may take their own lives or lose them to starvation or malnutrition——but I stand fast with those who courageously opted to shut down the economy in order to save lives.

In short, except for those who seek refuge in hoarding toilet paper and other essential goods, we have been hurled into a confrontation with mortality, with finiteness: our own and those we love. The specter of death has always put into sharp relief what it is we truly value, what matters most to us. To wake up is to live more deliberately, more consciously, more lightheartedly, and *that* is the hidden blessing behind this otherwise horrible crisis the entire world is facing. Humanity will survive this pandemic, as most of my beloved relatives did during the Spanish flu of 1918; the question is: Will the crisis bring us all together? Though I may be skeptical, It nonetheless remains my heartfelt longing.

Robert Epstein
El Cerrito, CA
2 June 2020

I am a firm believer in the people.
If given the truth, they can be depended
upon to meet any national crisis.
The great point is to bring them
the real facts.

~ Abraham Lincoln

Pandemic Haiku

Poems

Peril

quaking aspens ––
I don't want to die
on a ventilator

frightened senior ––
I ask him to hold his
60 year old teddy

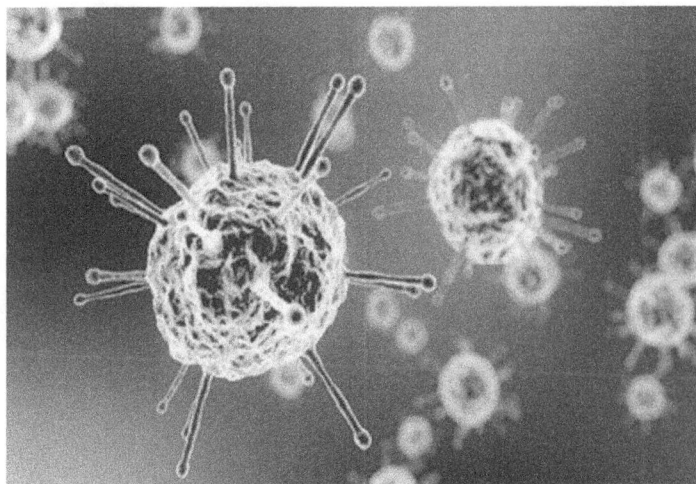

coronavirus scare --
the jogger running
faster than usual

not another poem
about cicadas
PPE shortage

we too are falling now with the honeybees

infections update
the sound of a frog
freer than we are

testing, testing . . .
testing alone is not going
to save us

he'll say almost anything the pandemic-in-chief

not ghosts or spirits
patients grasping at life on
ventilators

coronavirus scare ––
I think it's time
for holy basil

feared shortages ––
she heads to the nursery
for lettuce

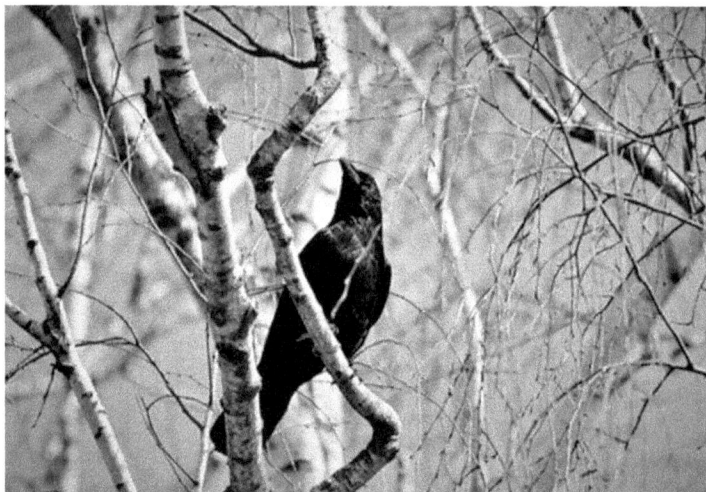

sheltering in place ––
out the bedroom window
the shadow of a crow

the front door shuts by itself pandemic

national emergency ––
she stocks up
on cookies

3,000 miles between us
my close friend and I
the same cough

whatever weather
every trip to the store
Russian roulette

pandemic ––
it doesn't help
with weight loss

days run together
I listen to the requiem
of my former life

pandemic morning
my neighbor on another
toilet paper run

at the food store pandemic paranoia

way past daybreak the porch light on the pandemic

coronavirus fears --
what a bowl of pea soup
does for the soul

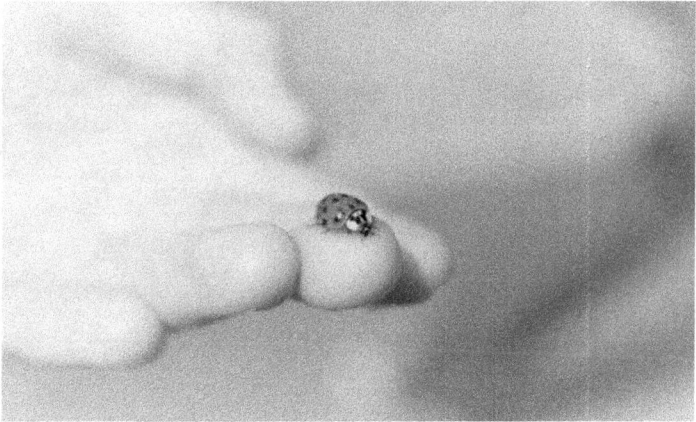

self-isolating
I let a ladybug
get close

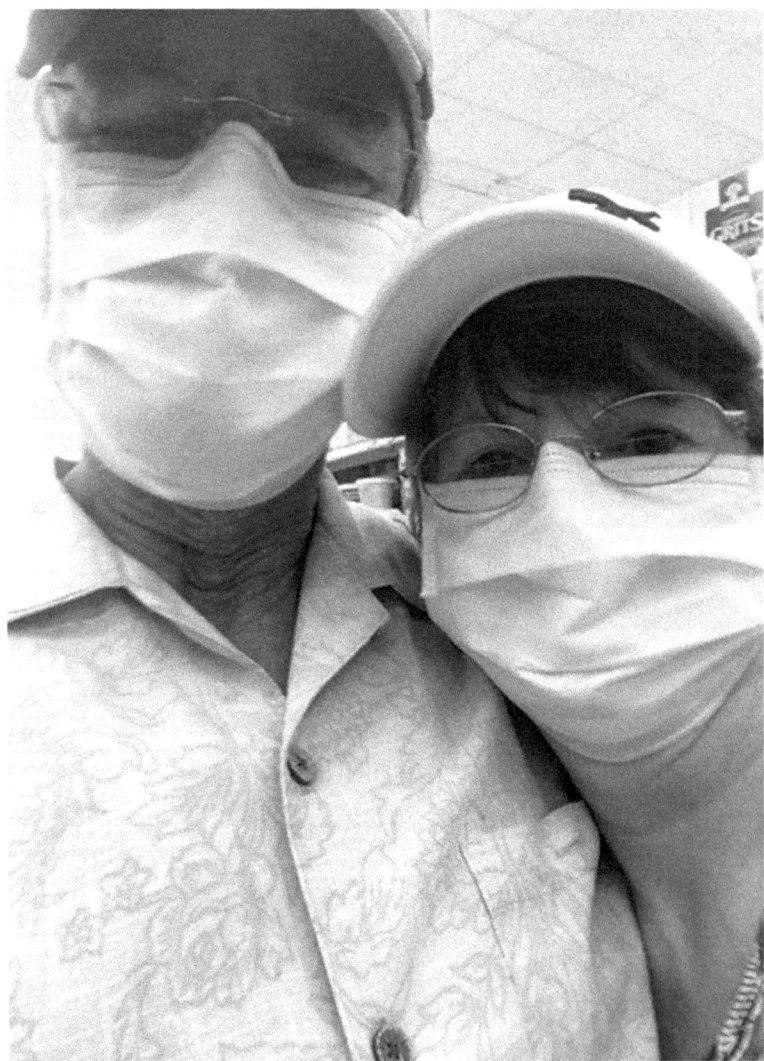

~ Photograph courtesy of Rocco Randazzo

face masks --
now we all look
like thieves

pandemic delivery
the toilet paper
under heavy guard

protesters ––
do they really mean *give me
liberty or the virus?*

saving lives
or sacrificing jobs
that is the question

losing the virus
deep in the black hills
of my psyche

before dawn ––
a new silence masticates
the pandemic

more cases confirmed
I continue to count
my blessings

pandemic testing the limits no-birth, no-death

the silence of dust
could these be
our last days?

coronavirus scare ––
I listen more closely
to buddha's breath

Impact

weeks at home. . .
how much I miss a simple
handshake, a warm hug

coronavirus --
who taught the mourning dove
to social distance?

waiting

for the market rebound

this sliver of sun

antibodies. . .
the landlord won't budge
on the rent

overcast day --
once more I befriend
dead writers

death tolls rise
the rain changes
nothing

sheltering in place --
still swiping
her dating app

Easter Sunday ––
no coughing during
the online mass

long March day
her offer of help
a week from *never*

to flatten the curve
I forage in the fridge
66th birthday[1]

just your run-of-the mill pandemic birthday

66th birthday
an old friend asks if I am
partying in place

twirling in the yard
in lockdown mode
my 66th birthday

~ *after Martin Epstein*

visualizing
a restaurant with cake
pandemic birthday

is it over yet?
not the pandemic
my birthday

media overload --
she turns back
to her cereal box

the pandemic
turning one and all
into shaggy hippies

if you blame the Chinese
for the pandemic
does that bring back the dead?

both famous

and anonymous

the coronavirus dead

Opportunity

waking up again
to his chanticleer
Walden

every morning
I open the blinds
to another future

how happy
the introvert is
having to stay home

sheltering in place --
a local woodpecker
brings us together

homebound --
the house is not cleaner
just brighter

self-isolating
I finally get caught
up on the laundry

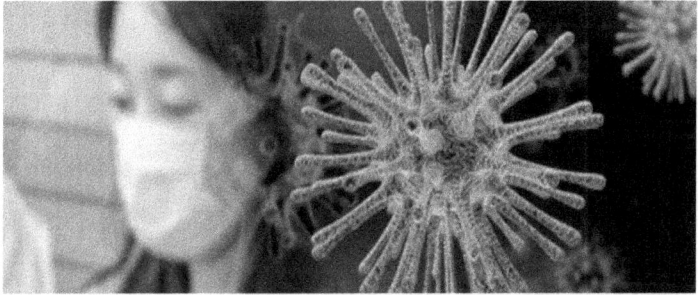

behind that mask
I know you are in there
as I am in here

self-isolation
I emulate
the scarecrow

MLK, Jr. --

I have a dream

he is back

for the first time
the freeways truly free
of traffic

takeout only ––
one restaurant patron leaves
a $3K tip

pandemic Monday --
how much of your life
is in order?

coronavirus scare --
she recommends a birdbath
for company

Zoom conference
how much I prefer
heard community

uncertain future
I rest my head on a stream
of moonlight

do not go
gentle into
the COVID night

~ after Dylan Thomas

making a pot
of disinfectant
I stop the pandemic

~ after Paul Reps

right here --
take a moment of silence
for the pandemic dead

listening deeply
after the recession
the resuscitation

the silence of dust
these could be
our last days

sheltering in place
the heirloom I will pass on
my neighbor's lemon

everywhere at once
Buddha with the smile
of unbearable compassion

Appendix A:

Pandemic Perseverance

coronavirus scare ––

the morning star

still enough

sheltering in place ––

she lip-syncs

through the day

coronavirus scare ––

my niece tells the ducklings

to stay in the creek

more cases confirmed

I continue counting

my breaths

coronavirus outbreak ––

in the dead of night

I clasp my two hands

the same walk ––

so many passersby

say hello now

COVID-19 spread ––

a neighbor's free lemons

flavor my soul

food store checkout ––

the worker hands each shopper

a spray of daffodils

high in the hills

a stranger meditates

the coronavirus away

Note

1. Please note that I have been a vegan for spiritual and ethical reasons for 45 years. The contents of the refrigerator in the photograph on page 48 are for illustrative purposes only and do not reflect my long-time dietary habits in any way.

When written in Chinese,
the word 'crisis' is composed
of two characters.
One represents danger and the other
represents opportunity.

~ John F. Kennedy

Stay Resilient,

Stay Safe